NINETEEN WAYS OF LOOKING AT AWONO

GEORGINA COLLINS

NINETEEN WAYS OF LOOKING AT AWONO

A POEM IN TRANSLATION

First published in Cameroon in 2024

Copyright © 2024 by Georgina Collins

The copyright of each translation in this collection remains with their individual translators or co-translators.

This publication is made possible, in part, thanks to support from the European Research Council and the University of Bristol.

All rights reserved. No part may be reproduced, stored in any retrieval system, transmitted in any form or by any means electronic or otherwise, without prior permission from the publisher, nor be otherwise circulated in any form of binding or cover than that in which it is published and without a similar condition including this condition being imposed on the subsequent purchaser.

Bakwa Books
PO Box 30056 Yaounde

www.bakwabooks.com

Print ISBN: 979-8-9872914-5-0
eBook ISBN: 979-8-9872914-6-7

Cover design by Elsa Westreicher

CONTENTS

Introduction i

The Poem: Le poème de Yambacongo | JEAN-CLAUDE AWONO 1

19 Ways: 4

1. Yambacongo's Poem | NFOR E. NJINYOH 4
2. Fi Yambacongo Poem | ELIZABETH (BETTY) WILSON 6
3. Yambacongo Poem | JEAN ANDERSON 9
4. Yambacongo's Poem | KAREEM JAMES ABU-ZEID 11
5. The Poem of Yambacongo | ALYSSA SALZBERG 14
6. Poem of Yambacongo | BONNIE CHAU 16
7. Ask Yambacongo | JK ANOWE 18
8. Yambacongo Poem | JOHN T. GILMORE 20
9. Yambacongo's Poem | PRUDENCE LUCHA 22
10. The Bandama Flow | GEORGINA COLLINS 26
11. Da poem o Yambacongo | CHRISTINE DE LUCA 29
12. The Poem of Yambacongo | N. KAMALA 32
13. Yambacongo's Poem | AILEEN RUANE 34
14. Ze Lyrik off Shtetlbetty | SOPHIE HERXHEIMER 36
15. The Yambacongo Poem | KHADIJAH SANUSI GUMBI 38
16. Story of the Stolen Creel| SARAH ARDIZZONE & ROHAN AYINDE 40
17. Yambacongo Poem | STEPHANIE SMEE 44
18. Yambacongo's Poem | MARY NOONAN................................. 46
19. Thothokiso ea Yambacongo | MANEO MOHALE 49

Afterword | KADIJA SESAY 51

Biographies 55

Acknowledgements 61

To the translators and other writers I have met along the way.

"Poetry is not only dream and vision; it is the skeleton architecture of our lives."

Audre Lorde. *The Black Unicorn: Poems, 1978.*

INTRODUCTION

Georgina Collins

> "Great poetry lives in a state of perpetual transformation, perpetual translation: the poem dies when it has no place to go."
> (Weinberger, 1987)

Poetry translation is an endeavour of passion, for it may bring cultural enrichment but seldom economic riches, the challenge once undertaken will likely be professionally rewarding but rarely satisfying as there forever seems to be a sense of incompletion… But never to translate the so-called "untranslatable," is never to attempt to communicate the unique stories of others, their values, beliefs, philosophies, histories embedded in a text. So how much more would be "lost in translation" (Frost, 7) if "great poetry" were not translated at all, and instead, were left to slowly fade away.

But fade away it will not as part of a seminal poetry translation anthology entitled *19 Ways of Looking at Wang Wei:* a book comprising 19 different versions of a short 4-line poem written during the Tang Dynasty (608 – 917 AD) by painter, calligrapher and poet, Wang Wei. Weinberger's petite 1987 book has shone a light on Wang Wei's poem for almost four decades now and is in its second edition (2016). I first read the text in 2005 on a Master's poetry translation option run by Prof. John T. Gilmore (featured in this collection) at the University of Warwick, and I have used it since in my own poetry translation teaching. Before *19 Ways*, I'd seen translation through the eyes of an undergraduate being tested on vocabulary and grammar. Weinberger's book opened my eyes to the irresistible number of possibilities in translation, and also to the challenges. Just one character in Chinese could be interpreted as three separate colours in the English language. So which would you choose and why?

Weinberger's book and Gilmore set me on a pathway leading to my keen interest in translating the culturally-embedded poetry of Francophone African writers. These two elements combined gave me the first glimmer of inspiration for this book: could I create something inspired by Weinberger, but with an African poet and cultures, centred around French and English and the multitude of different forms they take globally, one that explores current debates: creativity in translation, a more fluid 'original', the impact of identity upon translation, the judgement of translations (and the criteria we judge them against) and the relevance of 'The Death of the Author' (Barthes) to more contemporary literary translation strategies. Indeed, Barthes emphasised the reader's interpretation of a text as more significant to meaning than the author's so-called "intention", and as the translator is often the closest reader the text will ever have, should we see the source text as less of a straightjacket and more as inspiration for a new poem that allows what Weinberger calls the "spirit" of the source text to live on? In fact, this book could be seen as a translation of Weinberger's in that much looser sense. Here is a new version of *19 Ways,* this time 19 translations of "Le poème de Yambacongo" by Jean-Claude Awono.

I first met Awono in 2019 when working with the University of Bristol and Bakwa Books in Cameroon on a writing and translation workshop series. As Director of the publishing house, Editions Ifrikya, Awono had come to talk to participants about the literary and publishing ecosystem in Cameroon, and upon goodbye, he offered to send me some of his poetry. His work is predominantly free verse and highly embedded in Cameroonian cultures, history and languages. It is also very performative as he uses a plethora of sound devices (assonance, consonance, alliteration, rhyme, half-rhyme, strong rhythms, repetition, etc.) offering many a challenge to the translator. Awono is also a literary commentator, editor, teacher, and someone who has championed writing and poetry in Cameroon. Aside from being a remarkable read, his work also comes with a great deal of professional and experiential underpinning. Awono is also very open to translation, by that I mean he is interested in the process without expecting any particular outcome. Renowned—and widely translated—Ivorian writer, Véronique Tadjo holds a similar position on translation, stating that "a time always comes when I have to withdraw in order to let the text find its coherence and the translator his or her own empathy." This is rather like an open door to a translator; it is always helpful to have contact with a writer, but poetry is formed when it isn't constrained.

While reflecting upon Awono's work, I continued collaborating with colleagues from the University of Bristol as part of a team contributing to the ERC-funded project, *Literary Activism in Sub-Saharan Africa,* led by Professor Madhu Krishnan, an expert in African, World and Comparative Literatures. The team also included a group of cultural professionals from Sub-Saharan Africa, including Bakwa's Founding Editor, Dzekashu MacViban and Associate Editor and Senior Translator, Nfor E. Njinyoh. And it was on a joint trip to Senegal that I first mentioned the possibility of a *Nineteen Ways of Looking at Awono*. Making Black writers and translators more visible and highlighting linguistic diversity in literature are subjects that arise frequently in Bakwa/Bristol group discussions, so this book is a good fit and adopts an activist stance through the promotion of marginalised voices and languages.

In fact, I liaised with Dzekashu, Madhu and Nfor on the poem selection for this volume, deciding upon "Le poème de Yambacongo" for its evident abundance of cultural, linguistic and stylistic challenges for the translator. For example, how do we communicate the layers of meaning in the term "Ossimbi", the name of a district in a Cameroonian village (Guientsing I) close to Awono's village (Guientsing II), but also a word that sounds very similar to "guissimbi" meaning "soldier" in Nugunu, the language spoken in both places. This is just one of myriad considerations for the translators in this volume. Even the title of the poem warrants a conversation; take a look at the diversity of those translations on the contents page!

This anthology may be inspired by Weinberger's collection, but it is a very different book produced in a different climate for a different purpose. Obviously, the languages are not the same. French and English, the languages of this volume, are related Indo-European languages that use the same alphabet and have a number of true cognates, but the translation of Wang Wei's Chinese characters into a range of European languages is inevitably more complex from that perspective. What we do see with both collections is that cultural understanding makes a difference, but this is arguably more challenging in Awono's poem; it's much longer, and there are many more culturally embedded words, phrases and concepts. Weinberger's book also documents the passage of translation over time as the poems were previously published. Conversely, the translations in this collection were commissioned and have not appeared anywhere before.

Weinberger also carries out a (sometimes hard-hitting) critique of each translation, and we hear the voices of only a couple of translators (Octavio Paz and François Cheng, for example). As a translator myself, I found the latter process more insightful as it revealed the translator's strategy and reasoning. As a curator, I have chosen to focus more on giving the translators a voice through their commentary (also easier as all my translators are still alive!). Unlike Weinberger, I refuse to say what I perceive to be "good" or "bad" about each poem, instead I want to question the criteria used to form such judgements. Is a translation necessarily better because it is more closely related to the source text, more literal, the same shape, with similar sounds, rhymes in the same place? I prefer something more unexpected, innovative, imaginative even. In poetry, I see precision as an uncomfortable restraint, while others enjoy the challenge of exactness. Our judgement criteria are often personal, and timebound; translation trends and our expectations shift as the decades pass: domestication, foreignisation, literal, adaptive, and everything in between and beyond. Do we see a poem as a more fluid text, something related to oral traditions, thereby embracing innovation in translation rather than adhering to a more rigid notion of fidelity? Our stance is often related to the way we see our role as translators. Do we see ourselves more as scientific interpreters or artistic (re)writers?

The many possible voices of a writer in translation came to the fore after Amanda Gorman performed her poem at US President Biden's inauguration. It was commissioned for translation into many different languages, but a debate ensued as to whether the translators should also be young Black women with marginalised voices. The extent to which readers agree or disagree with that argument will vary, but what is most important, I believe, is that this news story highlighted to the general public the global lack of diversity in literary translation as well as popularising the oft-discussed issue of the translator's identity and the degree to which we need to share key demographics with the individual we are translating. Canan Marasligil elaborated on the subject to say that "A translator will make choices based on their life experience and their identity (so yes, race, gender, sexual orientation, religion, socio-economic background, disabilities… will matter)". Hence, this book tests that theory; to what extent and how does the translator's identity influence Awono's work in translation (without saying who should or should not undertake the task)?

When commissioning translators for this collection, I wanted to embrace a diversity of individuals and hopefully, therefore, to receive poems that sit at different points along the science-art continuum. Translators were approached to fulfil a few different and very broad criteria in terms of identity: a variation in terms of age, gender, geographical location, ethnicity, skin colour, education, profession, birthplace etc. We have not listed everyone's identifying traits, but some clues can be found in the translators' commentaries and biographies or are transparent in the poems themselves. JK Anowe translates into Nigerian Pidgin, for example, and Elizabeth (Betty) Wilson into Jamaican Creole. I invite the reader to reflect on all the translations and the connections between poem, language and identity.

The choice of translators was very organic; some translators I had worked with before or had met through studying and teaching in universities; I had read the translations of some and seen others perform their poetry; I approached people for recommendations, including editors at *Modern Poetry in Translation* and judges of the *Stephen Spender Prize*; I searched online, including on *Words Without Borders*, and spoke to friends in different parts of the world to seek out translators I had never come across before. All but three of those approached appear in this final version of the book, with time being the main reason why individuals were unable to contribute. Of the nineteen other translators in this volume, I have met just four in person. I am, of course, aware of a number of issues: that by no means can we claim to cover every aspect of identity in this small selection; that my own relationships have had a great deal of impact on the choice of poets; and that anthologising, in itself, is an inherently subjective process, even down to the order in which the poems appear in this book. For instance, I like the fact that Nfor E. Njinyoh helps us visualise the fish trap from the start, and yet Maneo Mohale's commentary is such a poetic and thought-provoking way to close the series of translations. I do not see this type of construction as a problem, so long as the reader reflecting upon the volume is aware that such a process has taken place.

Each translator was asked to provide a single translation of "Le poème de Yambacongo" in any version of English and using any translation strategy. As far as I'm aware, the poem hasn't been translated into English before. Translators were also asked to provide a short commentary. I did not want to lead the translators in any direction, so I waited to see if they asked me questions, if they had queries for Awono, or if they wanted his contact details. This did have an impact on my own translation as I was privy to more background information than I would ordinarily have requested. However, I did create my translation before I read any others. In addition, we were all aware that there were going to be eighteen other versions of this poem, and that certainly gave me more freedom, thus straying further from the source text than I may ordinarily have done. According to Weinberger, I'm the rebellious child that kicks back at the parent-original, while others may be overly-attached!

I was keen to include translators who take more of a source-focused approach than me—Khadijah Sanusi Gumbi, for example—alongside those who are more target-focused or take a creative approach. To some extent, we see this in Herxheimer's poem, which resituates many of the culturally embedded terms so that Yambacongo, for example, becomes Shtetlbetty. Nonetheless, we see both attachment *and* rebellion within most of the poems. Kareem James Abu-Zeid alters the register of the poem, beginning "What'd we do with it? / How'd we lose it?" and yet his use of a footnote reveals an intent to recommunicate as much source material as possible. Bonnie Chau translates the line-by-line structure of the source text, but not always the construction of individual phrases, for example, "Agad'Afouaga"—meaning "destroys-constructs" in Nugunu—becomes "Break-and-make-again".

In terms of experience, some contributors are regular poetry or literary translators, such as Mary Noonan who is also an academic, as is Professor N. Kamala and Khadijah Sanusi Gumbi, amongst others, but we've also included the work of a talented PhD student, Alyssa Salzberg, who offers a fresh nuance by gendering Agad'Afouaga as feminine. And there are writers in this volume who ordinarily do not translate Francophone literature, such as Maneo Mohale, an award-winning and multilingual poet. Some use versions of English that you may never have read before, like Christine De Luca's poem written in Shetlandic (a minority language and a variant of Scots that is related to Middle English) and then there is the poem by Sophie Herxheimer, who rather ingeniously translates into her German Jewish grandmother's English accent. Try reading it aloud! Others use more standard forms of English, such as Jean Anderson or me. However, this so-called standard language still varies from poem to poem; we all have idiolects governing our individual linguistic preferences.

We also have one officially collaborative translation from Sarah Ardizzone and Rohan Ayinde (I say officially as most translators ask for the perspectives of others), which brings a new dynamic to the poem, revealed in their commentary discussion. We also wanted to make sure we had at least two very different translators from Cameroon for an interesting comparison: Nfor E. Njinyoh and Prudence Lucha. Both draw on their childhood to support their choices in translation, and yet their poems are so distinct. Note the translation of "serpentaires" as snakebird by Njinyoh and serpent-eagle by Lucha. The list could go on, but essentially, identity, culture and the way we interpret our role as a translator, all have an impact on our strategy and choices, making every single poem unique.

The hope, then, for this volume is to create talking points that are cultural, linguistic, poetic, translational, personal and critical in nature. Kadija Sesay's thought-provoking Afterword begins that process. I am also keen for Awono's "great poetry" to have a new "place to go" albeit in many different forms, to be studied and to enrich readers culturally. And in a translation ecosystem that is increasingly influenced by Artificial Intelligence, the hope is that other literary enthusiasts might take inspiration from this collection and indulge in arguably the most challenging—but not impossible—task in translation: poetry.

REFERENCES

Frost, Robert, and Elaine Barry. *Robert Frost on Writing*. Rutgers University Press, 1973.

Marasligil, Canan. "Uncaring: Reflections on the Politics of Literary Translation". *Read My Week*, https://readmyworld.nl/en/an-editors-note/.

Tadjo, Véronique, and Kathryn Batchelor. "Translation: Spreading the Wings of Literature". *Intimate Enemies: Translation in Francophone Contexts*. Liverpool University Press, 2013.

Weinberger, Eliot, and Octavio Paz. *19 Ways of Looking at Wang Wei: (With More Ways)*. New Directions Books, 2016.

Weinberger, Eliot, et al. *19 Ways of Looking at Wang Wei: How a Chinese Poem Is Translated*. Moyer Bell, 1987.

THE POEM:
Le poème de Yambacongo | **JEAN-CLAUDE AWONO**

Qu'avons-nous fait du poème-ossimbi
Que Yambacongo voulut écrire
Quand dans le torrent du Bandama
Nous essayions la nasse brisée d'Agad'Afouaga

Ce matin-là
Nous étions allés plus loin que le trajet des pistes
Sur la forêt bavarde de Bahoya
Nous étions allés ramasser sur les plaines du Bandama
Les réponses à nos appels qui dans la nuit
Etaient tombées du ciel
Nous nous demandions ce matin-là
Quelle partie de la lune
Nous prendrions pour nos colins-maillards
A l'heure où la nuit comme un patriarche
Fait le partage de l'astre rond
Nous mirions sur l'onde crottée toutes nos têtes
Et nous souvenions de notre enfance
Qui passait sa vie à battre la rosée sur les sentiers
A célébrer l'ombre des serpentaires sur les voutes
A compter les empreintes des gazelles parmi la lisière des champs
A camper sous les safoutiers

Rien ne nous désexcitait
Et nous chantions la danse lente de la nasse dans l'antre hantée du Bandama
Et nul n'imaginait la transe épique et nouvelle du poème-ossimbi
Que Yambacongo voulut écrire
Quand sous le ciel accablé de serpentaires
Agad'Afouaga pleurait sa nasse

Aujourd'hui le ciel hisse sur des mâts
Des jours morts
Mais le lointain brimé nous pose toujours sa question endeuillée
Qu'avons-nous fait du poème-ossimbi
Que Yambacongo voulut écrire
Quand dans le torrent du Bandama
Nous essayions la nasse brisée d'Agad'Afouaga

"Le poème de Yambacongo" is a peculiar text. I don't remember exactly when or how I wrote it. But it is one of a handful of texts I wrote around the 2000s when I was a young teacher. It is therefore a poem, you might say, whereby the writing is anonymous, and its birth too was banal, ordinary, no cries, no drums, and no fuss… And yet, it is one of only two poems in my vast repertoire that I have learned by heart and performed fluently over the years.

Whilst I may no longer know precisely when and how I wrote "Le poème de Yambacongo", I do know why I did it… It was to avoid losing my childhood, my beautiful "kingdom", as Senghor taught us to call the morning part of our existential experience. It was to keep it fresh, in the poem's unalterable refrigerator. In the digital whirlwind of present times, with its volatile globality, we lose so many things, and one of the most fragile and most endangered is our childhood, our roots, all that was there when we began to form an awareness that we are confoundedly at one with light and darkness, but also with the ephemeral and the enduring.

How then can I not have within me a little of this Congo which first brought the reality of a proud civilisation in Central Africa to the world's attention? How can I not mention Yamba, the name inscribed in gold lettering on my paternal family tree, that of the great Gunu people in a country where the forest and savannah, the Mbam and Sanaga rivers forge an affinity between beauty and the unforgettable? Yambacongo is therefore a legendary figure of the poet's imagination, an organic mélange of unprecedented history and civilisation, a warehouse of anthropology laden with all the alluvial deposits of a past that is both familial and African.

I wrote this poem to say that not coming from your childhood does not mean that you come from somewhere else, but rather, you are succumbing to the sirens of nothingness and chaos. That is why, being a child of the forest and savannah, my poem is so full of water, of fishing, of fauna and flora, of forgetfulness and questioning, assonance and the land, blind man's bluff and the night, as well as the wild, noisy reverberations of words from the Nugunu language such as: ossimbi, agad'afouaga, bandama, bahoya…

It is a text that I do not understand myself, as its ambiance and depth go so far beyond any context formed by general truths and by my own truths. It talks of things as only souls inhabited by unspeakable and elusive sparks can do. I wrote this poem to call out the forgetting of time and of genesis. And so that forgetting falls silent on the threshold of speech. My childhood was too rich and very beautiful, and now cannot be forgotten in an imperishable poem.

Translated by Georgina Collins

1. Yambacongo's Poem | **NFOR E. NJINYOH**

> What have we done with the
> Ossimbi poem
> Yambacongo sought to
> forge as we wielded
> Agad'Afouaga's punctured
> fish trap in the hurtling Bandama
> waters?

At dawn, we had ventured beyond the footpaths into the wild, teeming Bahoya forest, setting out to the plains surrounding the Bandama to gather the answers to our calls, fallen from the sky in the dead of night. That morning, we pondered what side of the moon we would nest for the games that breathed life into our evenings at the hour when the night, like a wise elder, splits the celestial sphere into segments. We gazed at our reflections in the murky waters And reminisced our childhood; Lifetimes of feet brushing away dew along footpaths, mouths blessing the shadows of snakebirds perched in overarching trees; eyes investigating gazelle footprints in the vicinities of farms; hands foraging underneath fruit trees…

All was an invitation to excitement and discovery. And we sang to the slow dance of the fish trap in the haunted recesses of the Bandama. And no one could envision the novel, epic entrancing imperium of the Ossimbi poem Yambacongo sought to forge when, beneath the snakebird-infested sky, Agad'Afouaga bewailed his fish trap

> These days, the sky hosts lifeless days. Yet
> our hazed past whispers its forlorn
> question: What have we
> done with the Ossimbi
> poem Yambacongo
> sought to forge as we
> wielded Agad'Afouaga's
> punctured fish trap in the
> hurtling Bandama waters?

Growing up in a social environment where I often (rightly or wrongly) felt like a black sheep, most of my endeavours have always been plagued by a morbid fear of being misunderstood. This fear that sets me on a (self-imposed?) quest of avoidance of misunderstanding permeates practically everything, right down to my practice of translation, where I often end up dogging the source, my nose trailing its heel, finding it difficult to detach, lest I betray the source and beget a misunderstanding.

That was until I had my first go at literary translation several years ago with spoken word poetry. Despite the resolve to continue the quest, it became apparent that the tailing had to shift into dainty, Skopos-informed cat struts of some sort—a certain measure of constrained freedom.

Thus, trying my hand at this poem by Jean-Claude Awono—who admits not remembering the exact context within which he composed it—was an exercise in staying true to the spirit of his work, yet contriving an atmosphere to which any person who has experienced life in an African village can relate—from the farm-ward walks at the crack of dawn, through fishing in muddy waters, to bird-hunting with slingshots and evening games in moonlit compounds. Therefore, my final choices—right down to the fish trap-shape layout—draw from images of my own, eerily similar childhood experiences to attempt recreating and conveying the imagery, the feeling, the nostalgia that this beautiful poem evokes.

2. Fi Yambacongo Poem | ELIZABETH (BETTY) WILSON

Is what we did do wid de Ossimbi-poem
Dat Yambacongo did want fi write
When in Bandama rushing water
We was trying out Agad'Afouaga wicker fish-pot what Dem did mash up

Dat morning
We did go way way down past de whole length of de track-dem
Through de long tongue Bahoya forrest
We did go fi pick up pon de Bandama plain-dem
De reply to we cry
Dat did fall from de sky in de night
We was wondering dat morning
Which part of de moon
We was going catch fi play hide-and-seek
At de hour when de night like a grandfather
Was sharing up de round star
We was staring at we face pon top of de muddy water
And we member when we was small
And we spend we time a shake de dew from de pass-them
A celebrate de shadow of de serpent eagle-dem pon de heavens
A count de gazelle-dem hoofprint pon de clearing in de field
A camp underneath de plum tree-dem

Not a ting couldn't beat down we upfullness
And we chant de slow dance of de fish-pot in de haunted cave of de Bandama
And not a soul couldn't picture de epic and new trance of de Ossimbi-poem
Dat Yambacongo did want fi write
When Agad'Afouaga was bawling fi him bruk up fish-pot
Under de sky dat did dark wid de serpent eagle-dem

Today de sky hoist over de mast-dem
Day wat dead
But from far far de bruk down mash up horizon kip aksing us him mournful question
Is what we did do wid de Ossimbi-poem

Dat Yambacongo did want fi write
When in Bandama rushing water
We was trying out Agad'Afouaga wicker fish-pot what Dem did mash up

The poem is in standard French. I am bilingual in Standard Jamaican English (SJE) and Jamaican Creole (JC), often referred to in Jamaica as Patwa. This version of the poem is in Standard Jamaican English which I then "creolized" or translated into a more Creole form. Both SJE and JC draw on the same lexicon. Many Jamaicans move seamlessly between the two languages or mix them as we operate effortlessly somewhere on the continuum between SJE and JC. A version entirely in JC would be accessible only to JC speakers. Following the example of many Jamaican writers (Lorna Goodison, Pamela Mordecai, Velma Pollard, Olive Senior, for example) I have not used an official orthography for JC in my translation but used approximations spelt phonetically ("dat"/"de"/"dem") to represent our Creole speech. This has the advantage of making the poem accessible to a wider audience who do not speak or read JC. One final point: In JC past tenses and plurals are not indicated in the verb (e.g. by adding "-ed") or in nouns (by adding "-s"). JC marks past tenses or plurals in other ways: The boys = 'de boy-dem'; I wanted = 'me did want' or 'last week, me want', where there is no difference between the past and present tense forms.

"Tout traducteur est d'abord un chercheur"—Christine Durieux

The main challenge for me as an outsider who has never visited Cameroon, was to ensure that I understood the cultural content and context. As a Caribbean person, I am aware of the many pitfalls in translating an unfamiliar culture. I did research, consulted a Cameroonian resident in Jamaica, and then did the equivalent of a literary "analyse de texte". I do not believe the old adage that translations, like wives, cannot be both "belles et fidèles". Fidelity to the original author's version is as important to me as a felicitous translation, which conveys the message AND reads well. I try my best not to sacrifice either objective. I have had the good fortune to enjoy the cooperation of the writers I have so-far translated, and I know how important respect for their text is to them.

3. Yambacongo Poem | **JEAN ANDERSON**

What did we do with the Ossimbi poem
That Yambacongo tried to write
When in the fast-flowing Bandama
We tested the broken fishing net of Agad'Afouaga

That morning
We had gone further than the tracks traced
Through the speaking forest of Bahoya
We had gone to the plains of the Bandama to gather up
The answers to our cries fallen in the night
From the sky
We were wondering that morning
Which part of the moon
We would take for our blind-man's-buff
At that hour when night like some patriarch
Shares out the round star
We saw all our faces reflected in the sludgey water
And remembered our childhood
The years spent roaming the dew-damp paths
Celebrating the serpent-eagle shadows on the tree-tops
Counting the gazelles' tracks along the fringes of the fields
Camping beneath the butterfruit trees

Nothing brought us down
And we sang the net's slow dance in the Bandama's haunted lair
And no one imagined the new and epic trance of the Ossimbi
poem
That Yambacongo tried to write
When beneath a sky overwhelmed by serpent-eagles
Agad'Afouaga grieved for his net

Today the sky runs dead days
Up the flagpoles
But the bullied distance still asks of us its mournful question
What did we do with the Ossimbi poem
That Yambacongo tried to write
When in the fast-flowing Bandama
We tested the broken fishing net of Agad'Afouaga

A lesson in humility! So much in this poem that I didn't understand… I live in New Zealand but did this translation initially while staying with my daughter in Nouméa, so my access to resources was limited to what I could find on the internet. (As it happens, I am reviewing my comments again from New Caledonia, so the same restrictions apply…) As I specialise in Pacific texts, my knowledge of African geography and idioms is—as I was and am acutely aware—inadequate. Trying to pin down meanings took me down a few rabbit holes: 'battre la rosée', for example, evoked a Chinese proverb, which I hope I was correct to reject.

Because of my interest in and respect for (post)colonial writing I do tend to favour a source-text approach, which means that I am not averse to a degree of opacity in my final versions, and hope my readers share this approach. Like Edouard Glissant, I reject the idea that we must make everything crystal clear: there is a sense of domination in 'com-prendre' ('seizing', in Betsy Wing's translation) and I am generally content to 'simply observe', as it were.

However, had I known more about the context, I might have added a note or two… I sense some kind of dramatic event (political?) behind the 'childhood memories' theme. I have, as is my practice, tried to stay close to the original, while preserving its poem-ness: maintaining a degree of formality in the language without making it sound pompous was a challenge.

4. Yambacongo's Poem* | **KAREEM JAMES ABU-ZEID**

What'd we do with it?
How'd we lose it?
The Ossimbi poem,
the song from our village
Yambacongo had hoped to write
when, the Bandama flooding over,
we tried casting the threadbare nets
of *Agad'Afouaga*—
"rebel" and "renewer"
in our Nugunu tongue?

That morning
we went further,
walked off the beaten path
in Bahoya's noisy forest.
We'd gone to gather answers
that had fallen from the sky
on the banks of the Bandama—
answers
to our nocturnal cries.
We wondered, that morning,
what part of the moon we'd have
for our games of blind man's bluff
at the hour when night, like a patriarch,
doles out portions of the orb.
We candled all our heads on the muddy waves,
recalled our childhood,
the life that was spent
beating dew on the paths,
celebrating the shadows
of serpent eagles on the canopies,
counting the footprints
of gazelles at the edges of fields,
and camping beneath the safou trees.

Nothing could bring us down.
We sang the slow dance of the nets
in the Bandama's haunted dens,
and no one could've imagined

the exultation, the new and epic trance
of the Ossimbi poem, the one
Yambacongo had hoped to write
when, beneath a sky
overrun with serpent eagles,
Agad'Afouaga wept for his tattered nets.

Today, the sky hoists its lifeless days
on the flagpoles,
but the horizon, brutalized,
always asks us
the same mournful questions:
What'd we do with it?
How'd we lose it?—
the Ossimbi poem, the one
Yambacongo had hoped to write
when, the Bandama flooding over,
we tried casting the threadbare nets
of *Agad'Afouaga*?

---

* Translator's note: Yambacongo is a legendary figure originating in a song from the poet's youth that the children of his native village used to sing. Yamba is also the name of a distant figure in the poet's ancestral line, as well as one of the poet's uncles, and the name of a language spoken in Cameroon.

Evoking Loss, Translating Context

A successful translation first requires a clear vision or interpretation of the text at hand. In the case of Awono's remarkable poem, I found that the evocation of *loss*—the loss of the poet's childhood world—was central, and that the translation needed to hone in on and emphasize that aspect. This consideration governed most of my choices.

Once I'd completed a word-for-word rendition, I found that the aspect of loss was being overshadowed by a sense of confusion in the English, due to a lack of context. Context is a textual aspect that often goes untranslated, but I like to translate as much of it as possible, so long as it's not detrimental to the poem's flow. In the first stanza alone, we have several terms that are unclear in English, but that are meant to be evocative in the original. My online research of these yielded little clarity, but I was thankfully able to turn to explanations provided by Awono himself.

I intensely dislike footnotes for poems, but could find no other satisfying option for the titular "Yambacongo". For other terms, I made a couple of subtle and not-so-subtle additions to the text: "the song from our village", which is an inexact rendering of "Ossimbi" (which was, in fact, a village neighboring the poet's native village); and also the parenthetical paraphrase I added after "Agad'Afouaga," which means "he destroys, he builds" in Nugunu, but idiomatically denotes a rebel. With these contextual translations, I felt that the reader would be sufficiently oriented from the outset, and that the poem might now manage to make a real impact on the reader in English.

For the rest, I've gone with an American idiom, one that oscillates between a more colloquial register ("what'd", "how'd", "could've") and a more literary one ("threadbare", "candled", "exultation"). I've also used a fair amount of assonance and consonance (e.g., "portions of the orb") and even some weak or distant rhymes, and played around with various meters and rhythms—all of this to give the text a clear musicality in English.

5. The Poem of Yambacongo | ALYSSA SALZBERG

What have we done to the Ossimbi poem
That Yambacongo wished to write
When, in the flood of the Bandama,
We tested the broken creel of Agad'Afouaga

That morning
We had gone past where paths can follow
Through the chattering forest of Bahoya
Upon the plains of Bandama, we went forth to gather
The answers to our calls, which had fallen
In the night from the sky
We had asked ourselves that morning
What section of the moon
We would claim for our games of tag
At the hour when the night, like a patriarch,
Distributes the pieces of that round star
Our reflections would gaze back from the muddy shadows
And we would remember being children
Who spent our lives scattering the dew in our paths
Urging on shadows of serpent eagles across the rooftops
Counting the footprints of gazelles along the fields' borders
Camping under the safou trees

Nothing calmed us
And we would sing the slow dance of the creel in the haunted lair of Bandama
And none would imagine the trance, lofty and new, of the Ossimbi poem
That Yambacongo wished to write
When, under the sky crowded with serpent eagles,
Agad'Afouaga wept her creel

Today, the sky climbs the mast
Of dead days
But the subdued distance eternally asks us its mournful question:
What have we done to the Ossimbi poem
That Yambacongo wished to write
When, in the flood of the Bandama,
We tested the broken creel of Agad'Afouaga

This poem, embedded as it is in cultural context, was a fascinating piece to translate. The specific place names, the descriptions of the landscape and the wildlife, even the way the sky is described—the image we are given is specific, and I wanted to retain that specificity in the translation. I read a lot of articles and looked at a lot of photographs before I was satisfied with my translation; photos were a little difficult to find, but I was able to look through tourism websites, news articles, and satellite images to get a broad sense of the environment.

There is one word of this translation that gave me particular difficulty: *la nasse*. I opted, eventually, to translate this as *creel*, but this was a difficult decision. My hometown, Baltimore, is famous for its crabs, and these are caught using creels; it is a word and a concept I am very familiar with, and so it was the first one I reached for as an equivalent of *nasse*. However, after doing some research, I realized that crab and lobster creels are not quite the same thing as is referred to in the poem, although their definitions are nearly identical (i.e., a woven/netted fishing trap). A more precise translation would have been *weir*, but the word *weir*, which comes from Scots and Old Norse, struck me as very rooted in that part of the world. The same problem arose with *fishgarth*. Ultimately, I turned back to *creel*; not only does it fit the definitions of *nasse*, it also has the same musical feel to it. Both *nasse* and *creel* have something of the sound of rushing water to them, which is fitting for this poem. The original piece has a wonderful rhythm and sound to it, and it was very important to me to retain that. Another choice I made in my translation was to gender Agad'Afouaga as feminine; in making this decision, I wanted to preserve the personification of the original phrase, but doing so necessitated assigning it a gender. I try to implement feminist perspectives in translation when possible, hence defaulting to the feminine as opposed to masculine pronouns by translating *sa nasse* as *her creel*.

When a poem includes this many specific references, it can be daunting to approach it as a translator with an outsider's perspective, but good poems merit being shared, and that can often only happen through translation. The same way that stories in the oral tradition shift as they pass from mouth to mouth, poems shift in translation, but they do not have to be the lesser for it.

6. Poem of Yambacongo | **BONNIE CHAU**

What have we done with the poem-Ossimbi
That Yambacongo wished to compose
When in the flow of the Bandama
We were trying out the broken basket-trap made by Break-and-make-again

On that morning
We'd gone farther than the way of the trails
Over the forest rambling our Bahoya-banter
We'd gone to gather on the Bandama's plains
Responses to our calls which in the night
Had fallen out of the blue
We were wondering on that morning
What portion of the moon
We'd be given when playing blind-man's perch
At the hour when the night like a benevolent patriarch
Divides up shares of that rounded star
We looked into the muddied waves at our mirrored heads
And we thought back to being children
Our lives spent beating the morning-dewed paths
To greet the serpent-eagles' shadows on the canopies
To count the gazelles' footprints within the fields' edges
To camp out beneath the safou trees

Nothing diminished our energy
And we were chanting the trance of the basket-trap dance in the Bandama's haunted den
And we were none of us conjuring up the epic new daydream of the poem-Ossimbi
That Yambacongo wished to compose
When beneath the sky brimming with serpent-eagles
Break-and-make-again wept over his trap

Today the sky hoists up on poles
Days long dead
But the anguished horizon still asks its aggrieved question
What have we done with the poem-Ossimbi
That Yambacongo wished to compose
When in the flow of the Bandama
We were trying out the broken basket-trap made by Break-and-make-again

In the beginning, I thought: I am barely a translator, my French is lacking, I am a long-lapsed poet, I am an Asian American woman from Southern California living in Queens, NY. For a couple of weeks all I could do was carry around a printout of Awono's poem in my bag, reading it over and over, sometimes in my head, sometimes aloud, as I zigzagged my way around the city. I thought about the dynamics at play with language and colonialism in Cameroon, with the use of Bantu (Gunu?)-language words within the French, and when the question "Who am I to be doing this?" hovered over me, I felt encouraged, even emboldened, by the knowledge that there were eighteen others working on their translations as well, and that these translations would all be in conversation with each other, and with the original poem. Coincidentally, I also happened to be teaching Eliot Weinberger's *19 Ways of Looking at Wang Wei* in an undergraduate translation seminar—I was heartened by discussions with my students about self-interrogation, about how to read a work as a translator, how to read a translation as a translation, about the afterlives of a work that manifest in translations, about what can be triangulated by comparing multiple translations.

I could research serpent eagles and safou trees, but how much could I learn over the course of a few weeks about Cameroon and Bantu languages? I read about the agglutinative property of Bantu languages, that almost all words end in vowels. I went back and forth between verb tenses, I counted syllables, I consulted with a former student of mine who's from Cameroon, Tom Chiambeng. I tried for an openness, a looseness, a translation in which slightly different interpretations might shimmer depending on how a pause might take shape in the reader's mind, given the lack of punctuation. I tried to convey the elegiac tone and the musicality; the heartache that surfaces when distance from the freedom and exuberance of youth feels sharp; the pleasure of language and rhythm combining with image; the immediate immersion into a vivid environment, the sense of wonder tinged with hindsight, knowledge, time passed; the freshness and spontaneity in voice and movement that is both breathless and easy. In the end, "Agad'Afouaga," which caused me a bit of initial panic, perhaps turns out to be quite an apt way to think about the translation process—coming apart, constructing anew.

7. Ask Yambacongo | **JK ANOWE**

Wetin do awa orijinal pwem
Di won wey Yambacongo tok say him go write
Dat time for Bandama wen wata carry us
Enta trap wey Agad'Afouaga set

Dat morning
We waka pass wia we neva waka befo
Waka pass di tok-tok bush wia we bury di papa of awa papa dem
We say make we go Bandama go colect
Ansa wey folow sky come for night
Beht haw pesin won take esplain haw moon be
To pesin wey neva see am befo
Night divide moon like pesin wey get propati
We dey dey look am like wata wey won land for brain
E make us rememba wen we be small pikin dem
Wen we still dey use leg skatta dew wey dey road
Still dey hail animal wey cova sky wit shado
Still dey gist unda pear tree
Dey count antelope leg wey full field after antelope don pass

Notin do us
As we dance enta di witchi-witchi trap wey dey inside Bandama
E no geh anybodi wey fit imajjiin wia di eye of dis awa oji pwem see reash
Di won wey Yambacongo tok say him go write
Dat time wey feather full sky like wata full troat
Wey Agad'Afouaga crryyyy fo him trap wey break

Today sky still stand like electric pole
Wey we see yesterday
Beht na di same kweshun wey we ask befo we still dey ask now
Wetin do awa orijinal pwem
Di won wey Yambacongo tok say him go write
Dat time for Bandama wen wata carry us
Enta trap wey Agad'Afouaga set

The translation is rendered in Nigerian Pidgin English, the orthography of many English words altered to reflect their translated sound. This English is commonly prefixed by the adjective "broken" because it largely deviates from the formal grammatical structures of Queen's English. It is a language that first emerged as blunder, as misspeaking, as mispronunciation, so that "please" becomes "abeg" and "abeg" a portmanteau—I think—of the subject-verb "I beg". I imagine that a formal speaker of English, who has yet to experience this kind of interruption, could struggle to move through this translation. The grammatically minded person might argue that this is not how to correctly mispronounce or misspell in English.

Regardless of my speculations, I encountered these kinds of interruptions while reading the original poem; first, as a non-native speaker of French with an intermediate understanding of the language; second, with the presence of words whose meaning are not exactly accessible in the original language or in English. Words such as "Agad'Afouaga," "Yambacongo," and "Bahoya," because they are neither French nor English, opened a third dimension to my reading and translation of the poem.

The first dimension was translation from French to English. I started by creating a trot, translating each word independent of its correlation to other words in its line of origin. For example, my first translation for "Nous nous demandions ce matin-là" was "we we demand this/that morning-there" in place of the more grammatically correct "that morning, we asked ourselves…" or "we ask ourselves in that morning". The second dimension was translation from English to poetry. My plan was to take several liberties with the initial word-for-word disorder and reorganise everything into a more lyrically-sound grammar. I even translated "Yambacongo" as "country of the grassfield language" in one draft. Then, seeing the fragmentation in the trot made me realize that the words I couldn't translate worked in broken English as they appeared in the original poem.

In Pidgin, I am able to take a word specific to its cultural dialect and maintain the distance between that dialect and the French that comprises the rest of the poem. The intention, in part, is to limit the access of a formal English speaker the way the original poem might for a formal French speaker, opening it up to a reader even the poet may not have had in mind: an other living outside the grammatical constraints of standardized language.

8. Yambacongo Poem | JOHN T. GILMORE

What have we done with the Ossimbi poem
Which Yambacongo wanted to write
When in the torrent of the Bandama
We made our way through the broken fish-trap of Agad'Afouaga

That morning
We were going beyond the tracks
Which led through the chattering forest of Bahoya
We were going to gather up on the plains of the Bandama
The answers to our cries which in the night
Were fallen from the sky
We asked ourselves that morning
Which part of the moon
We would take for our games of blind-man's-buff
At that time when the night like a patriarch
Shared out the round star
We gazed at all our heads bobbing on the dirty wave
And we remembered our childhood
Passed in trampling the dew on the trails
Rejoicing in the shadow of the serpent-eagles in the over-arching forest
Counting the tracks of the gazelles along the tracks of the fields
Camping under the safou-trees

Nothing distracted us
And we sang the slow dance of the fish-trap in the haunted hollow of the Bandama
And no one imagined the trance, epic and new, of the Ossimbi poem
Which Yambacongo wanted to write
When in the sky overwhelmed with serpent-eagles
Agad'Afouaga wept for its fish-trap

Today the sky hoists on masts
Days which are dead
But the oppressed distance still asks its mournful question
What have we done with the Ossimbi poem
Which Yambacongo wanted to write
When in the torrent of the Bandama
We made our way through the broken fish-trap of Agad'Afouaga

My experience of translation (as opposed to the teaching of history and theory of translation, which I have often found to be something quite different) has included both purely utilitarian and literary translation. For some years now, my work on the latter has focused on the translation of Neo-Latin poetry, mainly from the eighteenth century. This has involved thinking about problems of form, and attempting to reproduce the self-conscious artificiality of Neo-Latin poetry by using strict verse forms in English. Something like "Le poème de Yambacongo", written in free verse, presents a different sort of challenge, and I am not sure to what extent I have managed to capture Awono's tone.

There are also issues surrounding both details of language and culturally specific items. While I have read a lot of French over the years, this has focused mainly on seventeenth- and eighteenth-century French literature, and, to some extent, the literature of the Francophone Caribbean, and I cannot claim any familiarity with Francophone African literature.

Online searches can help to some extent: I was able to find some information and pictures about *serpentaires* and *safoutiers*. I was going to call the *nasse* a "fish-pot", rather than a "fish-trap", as that is what items serving a similar purpose are called in the Anglophone Caribbean, but these are relatively small, whereas an online photo of a Congolese *nasse* shows an enormous structure across a river, which one could easily imagine youngsters picking their way through.

Context alone helps to identify the Bandama as a river, and I take it Yambacongo, Ossimbi, etc. are place-names. I couldn't find anything about Agad'Afouaga—there was an online reference suggesting it meant something like to destroy and rebuild, but I don't know how reliable this is. I am left thinking I am missing something crucial here.

The overall impression I get, and which I hope I have succeeded in conveying in my translation, is that Awono's poem is about how the exuberance and joy of youth is disappointed and frustrated as one gets older.

9. Yambacongo's Poem | **PRUDENCE LUCHA**

What have we done
With the ossimbi-poem
That Yambacongo wanted to write
When in the river of Bandama
We cast the torn cast net of Agad'Afouaga

That morning
We went beyond tortuous tracks
Through the talking trees of the forest of Bahoya
We went to the plains of Bandama
To gather answers to our calls
That in the night
Fell from the sky
That morning
We asked ourselves
What part of the moon
We would take for our hide-and-seek
At the time when the night
Like a patriarch
Shares the round celestial pumpkin
Over broken waves we gazed at our heads
And remembered our childhood days
That we spent
Beating dew along footpaths
Celebrating the shadow of serpent-eagles on vaults
Counting the footprints of gazelles across farm ridges
Camping under plum trees

Excited, nothing could burst our bubble
And we sang
As we danced the slow net casting dance in the haunted cave of
Bandama
And no one imagined
The epic new trance of the ossimbi-poem
That Yambacongo wanted to write
When under the sky overcast by serpent-eagles
Agad'Afouaga cried for his cast net

Today the sky stretches over the masts

Of bygone days
But the shattered past still poses its soulful question
What have we done
With the ossimbi-poem
That Yambacongo wanted to write
When in the river of Bandama
We cast the torn cast net of Agad'Afouaga

Literary works are generally influenced by the author's background and personal experiences, and although I am Cameroonian, I still needed to research the poet and study the poem to know its setting and understand its literal meaning before translating. Awono appears to be reliving childhood experiences that took place in a rural environment, and he poses a problem of poetic talents in young people that are often ignored and not nurtured. My research and understanding led to the following translation decisions:

- Jean-Claude Awono was born in 1969 at Sa'a in the Centre Region of Cameroon, and as Sa'a is known for its forest and serpent-eagles are snake-eating forest eagles, I translated "l'ombre des serpentaires" as "the shadow of serpent-eagles".

- My translation targets English-Speaking Cameroonians, particularly those from the North West and South West Regions. So, I translated "des jours morts" as "bygone days" and not "ghost days" because the latter may be misinterpreted as 'ghost town days' of civil disobedience within the context of the Anglophone crisis.

- This poem made me to relive my own childhood experiences. For instance, I translated "le torrent" as "the river" and "la nasse" as "cast net" since we used to swim in a river while some boys used old cast nets to fish.

- I translated some words following the rhythmic pace of African drum beats while using the language pattern of my native tongue. For example, I rendered "le torrent de Bandama" and "les plaines de Bandama" as "the river of Bandama" and "the plains of Bandama" respectively instead of "Bandama river" and "Bandama plains".

- We believed, during childhood, that trees actually talked in the night, especially when the wind was blowing. This memory, together with the attraction of alliteration, made me to render "la forêt bavarde de Bahoya" as "the talking trees of the forest of Bahoya".

- I translated "les safoutiers" normally as "plum trees" because the alternative "bush butter trees" used by some of our grandparents is now obsolete and will not be understood by most contemporary English-speaking Cameroonians.

- I used repetition as a stylistic device to translate "Nous essayions la nasse brisée d'Agad'fouaga" as "We cast the torn cast net of Agad'fouaga". The word "cast" is repeated for rhythmic reasons. However, when reading the poem aloud, the intonation of the first "cast" is different from the second one.

The poem does not have punctuation marks and I maintained that in the target text. However, in my translation, I split some lines or verses to create rhythmic pauses.

10. The Bandama Flow | GEORGINA COLLINS

Yambacongo
Yamba yambacongo'ooo
Calling out, recalling, crying
What became of the Ossimbi poem
You promised, you promised you'd write
Beneath past moons
We'd cast the fragile snare
Of Agad'Afouaga
Deep in the Bandama flow

That morning
We raced further
Than the pathway allowed
Among the babbling trees of Bahoya
And on the banks of the Bandama
Our calls had been heard
And we scooped up replies
Fallen from the sky
In the night

That morning
We pondered
Which part of the moon
We could pinch for our blind man's bluff
When the night soldiers
Would slice up the sphere
And our eyes stared back from the murky swells
Evoking adolescence
Spent trampling the dewdrops on the tracks
To see eagle shadows on the arches
To count gazelle hoof marks in the fields
To camp beneath the trees of safou plums

Nothing could stop us
And we sang a sleepy dance in the Bandama's darkened nest
The snare our inspiration
And never imagined such heroic exaltation
Or narration of the mutinous poem Yambocongo longed to write
As Agad'Afouaga bewailed his beaten snare

Beneath the eagle-sodden sky

Now
The blue flutters the dead days
On flagpoles
But torturous time forever poses that grieving question
What became of the Ossimbi poem
Yambacongo wished to write
Beneath past moons
We'd cast the fragile snare
Of Agad'Afouaga
Deep in the Bandama flow

Poetry translation is like the art of kintsugi; a beautiful pot, broken, then pieced back together with gold; a wonderful poem, fragmented then reconstructed with new sounds and expressions. Similarities exist but the poem will never be the same, instead the gilded words of another language allow the poem to live on. So, when I necessarily break apart a poem for translation, I am instantly thinking of ways to bring beauty back to it, always inspired but never constrained by the source text and writer.

I have few rules; for me poetry translation is about feeling a text, intuiting a writer and the creativity they bring to the page, to my senses and to my own imagination. I felt an instant connection to Awono's poetry; I was transported into his world, his artistic mind through his words, and that, in turn, inspired *me* to translate or, to be precise, to write poetry.

I do have a process of sorts. Awono's work is highly oral, highly performative, so after an initial literal translation, I began to add in the sort of stylistic features he likes to employ such as alliteration, assonance, rhyme and repetition. Rhythms, in their plurality, are integral to his work; they alter throughout. So, I read his poetry aloud to feel the bounce of the words, the drag, the alacrity, the sharpness as it shifts. I don't replicate all these qualities slavishly; features don't need to appear in the same place. I'm seeking the overall texture of the poem.

I also think about culture, about history, about the multiple interpretations embedded in Awono's words. I kept the sounds of the Nugunu language, but the meanings of those words, understood by a minority, are instead echoed throughout the poem; references to soldiers, destruction, construction, rebellion, revolution and the insect's unbreakable nest, for example.

And the words that open the poem are not frivolous, they are Awono's words, used to describe the childhood song that, in part, inspired this piece. So, my poem may look and sound different, but it comes from taking every little broken shard and patchworking them all back together with my own hands, and hopefully something glossy and new to hold the poem together, the breakage and repair just part of this poem's history rather than something to hide.

11. Da poem o Yambacongo | **CHRISTINE DE LUCA**

Whit ir we dön wi da Ossimbi poem
da een dat Yambacongo wantit ta write
whin i da Bandama torrent
we sowt da brucklin net o Agad'Afouaga.

Dis moarnin
we'd gien farder alang da garrulous gaets
an spaeky trenkies o da Bahoya forest.
We'd gien ta hent fae da plains o Bandama
da messages dat owrenicht wis faa'n fae da lift.
We windered dat moarnin
whit piece o da mön
we would tak fir wir trivvelin games
at a time whin da night laek a wise aald faider
shares da sun wi da tidder side o da aert.
We wir mindin on da möldy waves we wirkit,
aa da boannie heads o wis bairns
dat passed wir days guddlin i da dewy gutter apö da gaets,
celebratin da shadow o snakes i da rivvicks,
coontin cliv-metts o gazelles alang aedges o mödows,
campin anunder da berry bushes.

We wir nedder up nor doon, waitin
an singin da slow dance o da net i da oorie böl o da Bandama.
An naeboady imagined da new an epic draem o da Ossimbi poem
dat Yambacongo wantit ta write
whin, anunder da lift alive wi serpents,
Agad'Afouaga gret at his net.

Daday da lift heists bygone days
apö masts. But da far horizon,
dinged inta da distance, aye akses wis his unanswered question:
Whit ir you dön wi da Ossimbi poem
dat Yambacongo wantit ta write
whin, i da Bandama torrent,
we sowt da brucklin net o Agad'Afouaga.

This translation is in Shaetlan (Shetlandic), the language of the Shetland Isles, Scotland. I was born and brought up there so it is my mother tongue.

The rugged landscape of this island group at 60° North, with ever-present maritime influences—not to mention a cultural and linguistic heritage as much Scandinavian as Scottish—is in stark contrast to equatorial Cameroon with its forests, powerful rivers and coastal plains; not to mention its rich history. But there were similarities too: both communities of childhood memory worked small-holdings and fished; and both suffered language attrition (that net).

My main aim was to be as true as I could to the poem and, where that was tricky, to approximate to the meaning and enjoy the difference, creating other meaningful sound patterns. I wanted also to demonstrate how versatile Shaetlan is, despite being a minority tongue. My schoolgirl French was useful, but in places I had to resort to a dictionary and online translation of specific phrases.

Some ideas were fun to have a stab at translating into Shaetlan e.g.

> *... le trajet des pistes*
> *Sur la forêt bavarde de Bahoya.*

That adjective for 'talkative' allowed me to add a little alliteration:

> *alang da garrulous gaets*
> *an spaeky trenkies o da Bahoya forest.*

A 'gaet' is a path or way; a 'trenkie' is similar, but rather hemmed in.

'Nos colins-maillards' (blind man's buff) transformed into 'trivvelin games' (groping tentatively, as if blind), to retain the playfulness of the phrase.

I chose not to change *gazelles* to something more typical of Shetland as I rather enjoy the linguistic dislocation. But *safou trees* transformed into berry bushes.

Some lines I thought worked well e.g.

> *chantions la danse lente de la nasse dans l'antre hantée du Bandama*

which became

> *singin da slow dance o da net i da oorie böl o da Bandama*

A literal English version of that translation is:

singing the slow dance of the net in the eerie (animal's) bed of the Bandama

So while we don't have a Shaetlan word for 'lair', the next best thing was *böl* that place where an animal beds itself down. Sound-wise it also seemed to work.

12. The Poem of Yambacongo | **N. KAMALA**

What have we done with the Ossimbi-poem
That Yambacongo wanted to pen
When in the torrential flow of the Bandama river
We tried out the broken creel of Agad'Afouaga, a rebel destroying and rebuilding

On that morning
We had gone further than the track
In that chattering forest of Bahoya
We had gone to gather on the plains by the Bandama
The response to our appeal which had
In the night fallen from the skies
On that day we wondered
What part of the moon
We would take to play blind man's buff
At the moment when the night like a patriarch
Portions out the round star
We looked at the arc of our crocheted heads
And we remembered our childhood
That we spent stamping on the dew upon the trail
Celebrating the shadows of the Secretary birds up high
Camping under the Safoutier, prune trees

Nothing could dampen our enthusiasm
And we sang the slow dance of the creel in the haunted cave of the Bandama river
And no one could imagine the epic and novel trance of the Ossimbi-poem
That Yambacongo wanted to pen
When under the heavy sky laden with Secretary birds
Agad'Afouaga wept for his creel

Today the sky is hoisting on the masts
Dead days
But the harassed person faraway still asks us in grief the question
What have we done with the Ossimbi-poem
That Yambacongo wanted to pen
When in the torrential flow of the Bandama river
We tried out the broken creel of Agad'Afouaga

Translating "The Poem of Yambacongo" was a journey of discovery and delight. While Cameroon is not unknown in India, it is not as well-known as other Francophone countries. To translate the poem, it therefore required background reading to get to know the country, its geography and people.

The poem itself was like a stream flowing along with no punctuation marks to indicate any pause or direction, just as Prof. Njoh Mouelle mentioned in his preface to the poetry collection, *A l'Affût du Matin Rouge*. While this poem was clearly looking back at childhood, there were references and terms that were not so obvious to me, which the author so kindly helped in elucidating. I therefore wanted to clarify such terms for my readers as I thought that other people in India would also require a bit of clarity to enjoy the poem.

With this objective in mind, I set about translating it. I looked up practically every word that might be open to various interpretations or nuances before choosing to write what the poem communicated to me personally. Hence, I made additions in the poem, like the Bandama river, or trying to convey the multiple nuances of Agad'Afouaga, like a rebel destroying and rebuilding. Having attempted to introduce these shades, I did not reiterate them when the same words or references were repeated. Nonetheless, not every word was explicated, since I wanted to retain some of the mystery veiling the poem, e.g., the toponym Ossimbi did not contain any other shade of meaning than that of a village. At places, I preferred using what I thought was more poetic, like *to pen* instead of simply *to write*!

13. Yambacongo's Poem | **AILEEN RUANE**

What have we done with the Ossimbi poem
That Yambacongo wanted to write
When in Bandama's torrent
We tried to use the broken creel of Agad'Afouaga.

That morning
We went beyond the furthermost boundaries of the paths
Into Bahoya's chattering forest.
On Bandama's banks we had gone to collect
The responses to our calls that had fallen from the sky
In the night.

That morning, we asked ourselves
What part of the moon
We would clinch in for blind man's bluff.
At the hour when the night like an Elder
Apportions the round heavenly body,
We would gaze at the reflections of our heads in the thick waters
And remember our childhoods
Spent battering the dew on the trails,
Saluting the shadows of Secretary eagles on the canopies,
Counting the hoofprints of gazelles at the edge of the fields,
Camping out under the safou trees.

Nothing appeased us.
And we would sing the slow dance of the creel in Bandama's haunted cavern.
And not one of us envisioned the epic and unusual trance of the Ossimbi poem
That Yambacongo wanted to write,
When, under a sky overwhelmed by Secretary eagles,
Agad'Afouaga would grieve for his creel.

Today the sky hoists dead days on masts,
But the smothered horizon always raises its mournful question:

What have we done with the Ossimbi poem
That Yambacongo wanted to write
When in Bandama's torrent
We tried to use the broken creel of Agad'Afouaga.

"Le poème de Yambacongo" is a rare gift to study and translate. However, it is also a responsibility: Jean-Claude Awono's body of work is extensive, enduring, deeply personal, and far from my own lived experience. Embracing one possible feminist ethics of translation where "care" is privileged over political ideologies, I joined this project aware of my responsibility toward Awono's work. In practical terms, I chose to adopt a posture of humility—the poem is not my own. Nevertheless, I am choosing the words, the framework, and the rhythm through which this poem will reach its new audience. My feminist ethics of translation valorises the processes and collaborations (always implicated, but rarely vaunted) in translation work, and as such, my process has involved gathering background information about Mr. Awono's oeuvre, culture, linguistic environment, and poetics.

I was fortunate to be able to take advantage of information from Jean-Claude Awono, detailing the poem's context and themes. Learning about the different languages present in the poem, and how these interact via orality, helped to support certain translation strategies employed throughout the drafts, starting with a word-for-word translation and then progressing to the finished version. I would relish the opportunity to work closely with Awono in future: to bounce ideas back and forth and determine to what degree the rhythms of his poetry find their way into my English, which itself displays the intersections of Irish, American, and Canadian Englishes. Indeed, translation *is* creative, collaborative and productive work, and yet my feminist ethics of translation requires the translator to live the tension between proclaiming this creativity and honouring the source text's culture and author.

Translating poetry, especially that which privileges orality, is its own challenge. In this scenario, one possible feminist ethics of translation would recognize the importance of not overly assimilating the poem by translating with a goal of rendering it "fluent". This requires valuing difference, which entails not translating words in Nugunu: doing so means that readers will be able to glimpse the layers of influence that undergird the poem. But perhaps "glimpse" is the wrong word; in the end, I hope that they can hear the fundamental orality of Nugunu-influenced French as it finds a new existence in translation.

14. Ze Lyrik off Shtetlbetty | SOPHIE HERXHEIMER

Vot hef ve mait off zis Zeitzel-Lyrik
Ze vun Shtetlbetty vontett to ryte
Ven in ze Torrentz off Belaya
Ve tryte viz ze broken Netz off Glimt Gloom'nlendt

Zis ferry Mornink
So var off ze 'beeten Trex' ve strait
In ze chetterink Forrest off Shulgan Tasch
Ve vur goink to gezzer on ze Benkz off Belaya
Ze Responsiss to our Kalls vitch in ze Nyte
Fell from ze Sky
Ve voz vunterink zat Mornink
Vot part of ze Moon
Koot for our Blynte Mense Buff ve take
Et zat Auer off ze Paytriark-like Nyte
Vitch schairs ze Starse Rountnesse
Our Hetts togezzer resempelt a Vaif off Mutt
Ve remempert our Chialthootz
Ven we vekkt ze Dü from ze Parse
Selaybraytett ze snaykey Shettows in ze Kortyart Roofs
Kountett ze Pawprintz off Hayers ett ze Etchiss off ze Feelt
Kempt out unter ze Plum Treez

Nussink stoot in our Vay
Oont ve sengk ze slow Tantzis off ze Netz in ze horntett Kaif off Belaya
Nun off us imechint ze nü oont epik Trantz off Zeitzel-Lyrik
Zat Shtetlbetty vontett to ryte
Ven unter ze Snayke effliktett Sky
Glimt Gloom'nlendt vept her Netz

Today ze Sky hoists on its Rigkink
Ze Dett Dayze
But off ze supchukaytett Distentz ve still eskink ze greef-struk Kvestion
Vot hef ve dun viz ze Zeitzel-Lyrik
Zat Shtetlbetty vontett to ryte
Ven in ze Torrentz off Belaya
Ve tryte viz ze broken Netz off Glimt Gloom'nlendt

Reading the melodic swoosh of Awono's poem, its delight in a sonorous fluid French, and the way it is peppered with proper nouns, all of which appear a few times and form part of the rhythm and music of the poem, I was struck by the impossibility of the task awaiting me. I looked up the proper nouns and found few straightforward definitions; the Bandama is a river not in Cameroon, but in Côte d'Ivoire, who is *Yambacongo* who 'wanted to write the poem'? '*Agad'Afouaga*? A stuttering sound—resonant with its own unsayability, and I read in a piece about Awono, that it was a coded place name signifying destruction. Vell. My Chermen Chooisch Grentmuzzer in whose Inklisch I voz eskt to trenslayte, outseit off Europe she neffer set a foot! So if I was borrowing her voice to create a version of the poem, I needed to transpose it to her own mid twentieth century war torn Kontinent, so that it would be something and somewhere that she and her peers could inhabit. Her Lenkvitch is of the opposite aural world to the original poem—for every lush 'ou' sound, or long è as in *lisière*, *serpentaires*, the round sounds of *ombre*, *compter*, *camper* all in consecutive lines— which give the poem such swell, Inklisch would inevitably offer a much harsher soundscape: clicking and scratching through the lyrik like consonant based machine gun fire. I kept to Awono's form: the line breaks remain the same, the lack of punctuation, (though I could feel my Grentmuzzer object!) I replaced the river with one in Russia, and a forest that apparently grows beside it, I gave Yambacongo the name Shtetlbetty, implying a gender shift for the crowd in the poem, and shtetl to also suggest community/village in a wider European Jewish culture, rather than just the Saxony where 'Liesl' was from, though Zeitzel as in Zeitzel-Lyrik, is near Leipzig. I replaced the gazelles with hares. As ever, I favoured creating a sound world for the poem, musicality over a literal rendering. Glimt Gloom'nlendt felt like an equivalent for Agad'Afouaga, carrying some nonsense nod to destruction in the gloom, the land, the alliteration.

15. The Yambacongo Poem | **KHADIJAH SANUSI GUMBI**

What have we done with the poem-ossimbi
That Yambacongo wanted to write
When in the torrent of the Bandama
We tried the broken trap of Agad'Afouaga

That morning
We had gone further than the path of the tracks
On the chattering forest of Bahoya
We had gone to collect on the Bandama plains
The answers to our calls in the night
Had fallen from the sky

We wondered that morning
Which part of the moon
We would take for our collar-mallards
At the hour when the night like a patriarch
Shares the round star

We looked at the crumbling wave with all our heads
And we remembered our childhood
Which spent its life beating the dew off the paths
Celebrating the shadow of the snakes on the vaults
Counting the gazelle's footprints on the edge of the field
Camping under the safflower trees nothing could scare us

And we sang
the slow dance of the trap in the haunted lair of the Bandama's den
And no one imagined the epic and new trance of the poem-ossimbi
That Yambacongo wanted to write
When under the serpent-ridden sky
Agad'Afouaga wept for his trap
Today the sky raises on masts Dead days

But the distant and oppressed still asks us the mournful question
What have we done with the poem-ossimbi
that Yambacongo wanted to write
When in the torrent of the Bandama
We tried the broken trap of Agad'Afouaga

A journey of inspiration awaits in the works of Jean-Claude Awono, a Cameroonian poet whose words are both beautiful and thought-provoking. The poetic imagery he crafts brings to life a world of emotion, one that speaks to the human condition and challenges us to think deeply and reflect on our lives. The translation of Jean-Claude Awono's 'Yambacongo' from French to English is a delicate art, requiring a nuanced understanding of the poem's language, culture, and context.

As a Nigerian translator, I tried as much as possible to capture the essence of the poem while staying true to its original form and preserving the beauty and power of the poem in the target text. The poem 'Yambacongo' is a powerful exploration of the human experience, inviting readers to explore the depths of their own emotions. The vivid imagery of 'Yambacongo' resonates with readers, inspiring them to reflect on the beauty of life, love, and loss. This beauty is unparalleled, with its lush green hills, majestic waterfalls, and vibrant wildlife. It is a place of refuge and solace, where we can go to find peace and strength in times of need.

When translating 'Yambacongo' to English, it is important to have a clear understanding of one's objectives in the translation process. For me, these include the accurate conveyance of meaning and emotion from the original poem to the target text, while also respecting the source text context, including its culture.

I was also mindful of the poem's original tone as well as any features or nuances that may be lost in translation. I believe I was able to capture the text in a way that both respects the original language and the poem's beauty and emotion.

In conclusion, 'Yambacongo' is a very powerful poem that reminds us of the importance of understanding one's feelings and striving to find inner peace in a world that can often be filled with darkness and despair.

16. Story of the Stolen Creel | **SARAH ARDIZZONE &
ROHAN AYINDE**

What have we made of Ossimbi's song
written in Yambacongo's open mouth
the Bandama around us, dancing
as we plunged to free Agad Afouaga's stolen creel

That morning,
we crept through Bahoya's waking forest,
tasting the dew with our heels
and winding beyond the tracks we found
to greet the great Bandama,
answer to our prayers,
the night sky dropping
to meet us there.

We asked the moon, that morning,
which of its faces we could use
to play our blind man's buff
as night kissed sun
in the day's gathering, our faces hovering
in the churning water's hold
like memories of childhood
wet with dew beneath our feet —
when we danced under the shadows of Secretary Birds
making tracks beside gazelles'
before the afternoon's edge pulled us
beneath the shade of Saffron Plums

Nothing could still our excitement
As we sang the creel's slow dance,
caught in the dark echo of Bandama's cave

And none of us imagined how our breath
would soon become Ossimbi's song,
an epic trance in Yambacongo's open mouth when
under a sky aching with Secretary Birds
Agad'Afouaga mourned his creel

Today the sky wears the past like a sail
and those distant days insist in grief

What have we made of Ossimbi's song
written in Yambacongo's open mouth
the Bandama around us, dancing
as we plunged to free Agad Afouaga's stolen creel

Sarah Ardizzone (SA): Rohan and I have been collaborating, in different ways, since 2003 when Rohan was a teenage slang consultant on GOLEM, a multicultural children's series I was translating for Walker Books. Our most recent collaboration took place during lockdown and over Zoom, when we co-'voiced' Mehdi Mazouni, a feisty secondary school student in *Men Don't Cry* by French Algerian novelist Faïza Guène.

When Georgina Collins approached me about translating Awono, I suggested bringing Rohan into the creative process. In our combined approach to the Cameroonian French original, Rohan was keen to draw on his spoken-word poetry expertise, as well as his British Guyanese heritage—with me serving as a conduit/bridge translator/sounding board. We met up for two extended sessions: one more research-based, the second more editorial.

Rohan Ayinde (RA): To give some sense of process: for me, it's important to hold this notion of the story being told as timeless; bringing together past and future through the reflection of this one specific story. There are the rich overlapping meanings and doubling of the words in the original. Also, the rhythm and cadences of the poem: I'm not trying to recreate them, but to find the musicality in my own writing. I'm constantly reading the poem back to myself—in this way the music is always in my mouth. The language is 'becoming' not just on the page but also in my breath.

SA: I'm loving the energy and freedom of your flow. So, there's an interesting creative tension for us here—positive friction, if you like: between you as the poet (this is categorically *your* poem) and me as the translator asking questions in the vein of "are you carrying enough over?"

RA: I'm more interested in the poem feeling true to the original than I am in it being as close as possible to what Awono wrote. Of course, the feeling is completely subjective to each reader and their experiences.

SA: Who are you writing for?

RA: There's a part of me that's writing for the original poet. Am I able to capture enough? With Awono, looking at the dance… at the sense of place… I wanted to capture someone reflecting on childhood in a way that resonates. For me, that's about growing up on the Tulse Hill estate: moments of childhood when you're learning about yourself, manhood and comradery. Awono took me to poems that I've written about those things. I was seeking out the point of connection between playing football in the cage on the Tulse Hill estate and tracing the tracks of gazelles on the plains of the Bandama. Wildly different but not so different… Take the idea of going beyond the tracks of elders—it's an expression of the boyhood urge to go beyond what people have made in your community.

17. Yambacongo Poem | STEPHANIE SMEE

What did we do to the Ossimbi poem
That Yambacongo wanted to write
When in the rapids of the Bandama
We tested the broken trap of Agad'Afouaga

That morning
We had ventured further than the paths leading
Towards the gossiping forest of Bahoya
We had gone to gather on the plains of the Bandama
The answers to our calls
Fallen from the night sky
We wondered that morning
Which side of the moon
We would use for our blind man's buff
When night like a patriarch
Divided up that round star
We gazed at ourselves
All our faces reflected in the muddy swell
And remembered childhoods spent
Tramping dew from the paths
Marvelling at shadows cast by secretary birds against the vaulted heavens
Counting gazelle tracks at the fields' edge
Camping under the safou trees

We would not be subdued
And we would sing of the trap's slow dance in the Bandama's haunted lair
And nobody imagined the epic new trance of the Ossimbi poem
That Yambacongo wanted to write
When under a sky weighted with secretary birds
Agad'Afouaga lamented his trap

Now lifeless days are hoisted skywards on masts
But the tormented past
Still questions us in its grief
What did we do to the Ossimbi poem
That Yambacongo wanted to write
When in the rapids of the Bandama
We tested the broken trap of Agad'Afouaga

I have always maintained that in order to translate poetry successfully, one must be a poet oneself. I am not a poet. I have had the great privilege of translating Joseph Ponthus' prose poem, *À la ligne: Feuillets d'usine* (Editions de La Table Ronde, Paris, 2019), which posed a great number of challenges, yet still I shy away from calling myself a poet.

Rereading *19 Ways of Looking at Wang Wei*, I came across Weinberger's comment about one rendition of Wang Wei's poem as "a classic example of the translator attempting to 'improve' the original". In its way, Weinberger says, translation is "a spiritual exercise, [...] dependent on the dissolution of the translator's ego: an absolute humility toward the text." I am not fond of absolutes. But humility is always a useful starting point, an assumption that the author's choices are deliberate, intentional.

So, what to make of the unfamiliar proper nouns in an English translation? No fewer than four in the first stanza! What is the translator's role here? Surely many readers of the original French would be as baffled by these references as readers of its translation here in Australia. But poetry and footnotes make for uncomfortable bedfellows. I understand that *Agad'Afouaga* is a composite noun from two verbs: *he destroys/he builds*, yet few French speakers would have access to this meaning in the original either. Is it the job of the translator to 'clarify' in the body of the poem? I don't believe it is.

And what to do with *poème-ossimbi*? Reference to this line in another source revealed it to be written *poème Ossimbi*, capitalised and unhyphenated, but pointing more obviously to the name of a village in Cameroon.

Translators make micro-decisions at every turn. We find ourselves (usually) alone with the text, often besieged by doubts, wondering at the possibilities, questioning whether our decisions even matter. But always we are listening for rhythm, for musicality, looking for patterns, hoping humbly to reflect the author's deliberate intent. And fervently hoping readers consider not only what has been lost, but what has been found.

18. Yambacongo's Poem | **MARY NOONAN**

What have we done with the ossimbi poem
that Yambacongo wanted to write
when we were fishing in the fast-flowing Bandama
with Agad'Afouaga's broken keepnet?

That morning
we went beyond the dust tracks
through the noisy Bahoya forest
We went to collect our booty
on the plains of the Bandama –
the answer to our prayers had appeared
out of nowhere in the night
That morning
we wondered which part of the moon
we'd take for our blind-man's-bluff
At that early hour, when night the patriarch
divides up the round star
we were gazing at each other's heads
bobbing in the muddy water
and remembering our childhood,
the days spent flattening the dew on dirt tracks
and singing the praises of the shadows of secretary-birds
on the mountains and counting the prints of gazelles
at the edge of the fields. And camping out under
the plum trees

Nothing could tame our excitement
and we danced the slow dance of the net
in the haunted lairs of the Bandama
And no-one could have imagined the epic
trance of the ossimbi poem that Yambacongo
wanted to write when, under a sky heavy
with secretary birds, Agad'Afouaga cried for his net

Today the sky hoists only dead days
on its masts, but the bruised faraway is still

asking its grief-question:
What have we done with the ossimbi poem
that Yambacongo wanted to write
when we were fishing in the fast-flowing Bandama
with Agad'Afouaga's broken keepnet?

The most immediate effect the poem had on me was that of plunging me into a feeling of strangeness—of the uncanny, almost. There are a number of mysteries in the poem that I couldn't solve. When translating a poem that has elements that may have come directly from the poet's unconscious, the task for the translator is to remain faithful to this mood and tone of strangeness. The temptation may be there to 'interpret' the poem, to make its meaning more accessible to the reader. In translating Yambacongo's Poem, I could see that whenever I did interpret the meaning, I was immediately making the poem a little more banal, losing the marvellous quality of enigma of the original, where the reader is plunged into a breath-taking, unfamiliar experience.

Also in keeping with this feeling of interruption or disturbance, place and time are not stable in the poem. The poem moves from the present to the past ('Ce matin-là) and then back further to the more distant past, to childhood. The reader/translator is struggling with these layers of time, trying maybe to locate them chronologically. The sustained use of the imperfect tense in French is somewhat unusual, and is clearly meant to bring the reader directly into the aliveness of the past scene that is being evoked. But English poetry is not fond of a sustained present participle or gerund, so translating these verbs is a challenge.

The wonderful names—Yambacongo, Agad'Afouaga, Bandama— add to the English reader's sense of displacement. I began by trying to understand if the names referred to people or places. And then there are the marvellous 'serpentaires'. When I looked in the dictionary, I found both 'secretary bird' and 'serpent eagle'. Further research revealed it was more likely to be 'secretary bird', which I discovered are very tall birds of prey with a fabulous crested tuft on their heads, very long legs and a powerful wing-span. They hunt just after dawn, which ties in with the narrative of the poem. The poem transports the European reader to a place where hardly anything is familiar.

Therefore, I must conclude that the poem is undoubtedly following a tradition that, living in Ireland, I'm not familiar with. I tried to remain true to the style and lay-out and dream-like logic of the original, and not to force it into a Western corset. I wasn't always successful in this aim.

19. Thothokiso ea Yambacongo | **MANEO MOHALE**

Reentseng le pina ea ossimbi
That Yambacongo wanted to write
Nakong ea morwallo ea mo Bandama
When we tried the broken trap ea Agad'Afouaga

Hoseng
We went further mo tseleng
In the chattering forests tsa Bahoya
We went picking mo di jarete tsa Bandama
Bosiu, the answers to our calls
had fallen hodimong
Hoseng, we asked ourselves
Which part of the moon
Would take us ka bofofu
Bosiu, ha Bosiu, like a patriarch
shares the round star
Rona kaofela on the muddy wave, all our heads
Remembering our childhoods
Bona, who spent their lives beating the dew on the trails
Celebrating the shadow tsa linoha on the vaults
Counting the footprints tsa litshepe at the edges of the fields
Camping under the safoutiers

We were bored by nothing,
Ra bina slow dance in the haunted lair, metsing ea Bandama
And no one imagined the epic and new trance ea pina ea ossimbi
That Yambacongo wanted to write
Tlasa hodimo, when overwhelmed by snakes
Agad'Afouga a lla likeledi over his trap

Kajeno lehodimo hoists on masts
Dead days
Empa, the far off and repressed always asks us potso eo e bohloko
Reentseng le pina ea ossimbi
That Yambacongo wanted to write
Nakong ea morwallo ea mo Bandama
When we tried the broken trap ea Agad'Afouaga

Translating this extraordinary, haunting poem was a strange process. I struggled to find a way in, having last studied French in university. Like all my best endeavours, I approached translation collaboratively, enlisting the help of my chosen sibling, Elijah Ndoumbe, a multidisciplinary artist with lineages connected to, and across West and Southern Africa, as well as the United States.

We exchanged and compared translations over email and WhatsApp, while I relied on my old dictionary, resulting in a fizzy and messy mother text. As an exercise in colouring the text with my own tongue, I imagined reading the poem to my grandmother. This grounded the poem immediately, where it began to take on both a geolocality, and a kind of rooted fleshiness, coloured by the green house in the East Rand of Johannesburg, South Africa, where she resides.

In speaking to her, I lean on Sesotho, my father tongue, though I speak a broken and clumsy liminal version of the language, heavily infected with English. The act of passing the text to her, through me, produced a kind of conversational poem. The poem makes both delightful and uncomfortable sounds. I found myself eavesdropping on the tension evoked by French and Sesotho's proximity, with my Sesotho-fied English acting as a messy mediator.

The resulting poem feels both talkative and elegiac, hybridised, and soaked in imagined time. A talking song. I find it interesting that even though this conversation is imagined, and touched by many black hands, it still cannot escape a haunted, colonial texture. Looking at the poem now, I'm thinking about translation as the transmission of story, a transmission that gives text both mass and texture, surrounded by the buzz of voices before and around and inside it.

AFTERWORD

Kadija Sesay

"'Who am I to be doing this?" asks New York based translator Bonnie Chau.

As the writer of the Afterword, I asked the same, immediately identifying with the first seven lines of her statement as I'm sure others will if they experience imposter syndrome. What I sensed from all of the translators was that they were honoured and humbled to be included in such a project; and that despite the challenge, which may have included being initially unsure about the final outcome, they were nevertheless going to take a personal approach that would synchronise with Jean-Claude Awono's "Le poème de Yambacongo" to create something deeply fulfilling. Whilst doing so, they would learn as much as the readers they were translating for.

Such a project takes some initial thinking about because as Bonnie Chau shared, it lived on paper in her bag for a few weeks. During which time, the poem probably also walked in her mind, changing direction when it wanted. Even if a translator has a preferred approach to translating poems, each poem they translate, has its own life, its own backstory, and at least a few layers of metaphor, context and points of entry. Each poem has to be approached differently too. For example, how much background research needs to be undertaken? How much of the poet's personal background is sought and considered; other works of the poet, the meaning of names and places, an understanding of gender? As a translator, do you genderise it like Alyssa Salzberg, who, "wanted to preserve the personification of the original phrase, but doing so necessitated assigning it a gender." She says she defaults to implementing a feminist perspective in translation, however and whenever she can. Each poem talks to you differently—and even more infuriating, it will talk to you differently on different days.

I also identified closely and immediately with JK Anowe, and his Nigerian Pidgin translation as well as Elizabeth (Betty) Wilson's Jamaican Creole one. As a Sierra Leonean Brit living in the UK, I am surrounded and am often in the company of these voices and Englishes. Over 25 years ago, Mark Sebba led a UK based Jamaican patois project titled "How do I spell Patwa" and gifted me with a link to all his papers on this project when he retired. In comparison, there is little such work on African Englishes spoken in Britain or, to break it down further, into London Nigerian Pidgin—different from Pidgin in Nigeria or Ken Saro-Wiwa's "Rotten English" which he creatively popularised (Tunca, 2009). So, when it comes to those people living in England using London Jamaican Patois or London Nigerian Pidgin, the English is different yet again (and notice how I've regionalised it, as do some of the translators in the book).

In my collection of poetry, *Irki*, the poems in my grandmothers' voices are written in Krio to incorporate the heritage of my grandmothers—neither of whom spoke English—and I had to interpret their lives, beliefs and feelings into voices. This included how they would speak to their children (my parents) and to each other. My paternal grandmother was Krio; my maternal grandmother was Mende—she didn't speak Krio but for the sake of the story, I re-imagined that she did—and so the Krio between them is different in tone and intensity. By intensity, I mean, how 'deep' is the Krio? as my sister-in-law refers to it. Because when she speaks deep Krio, I'm lost, as her speech is punctuated with proverbs that I haven't grown up with. Patois and Krio have gradually claimed to be their own languages, partly due to an urgent and necessary need to decolonise European languages and their derivations. Krio used to be referred to as broken English, too, but no longer. These various Englishes are more than linguistic and cultural excavations as they also factor in human geography since they denote the various ethnicities and population figures living in Britain. It also shouts loud to freedom of the tongue. I carried this in my head as I read about the challenges these translators faced.

This collection of English translations demands that the reader think of their own Englishes and how many they use without necessarily being aware of it. As Derek Walcott discussed on a television programme of Caribbean poetry (*Caribbean Nights*, 1986) with poets Fred D'Aguiar and Linton Kwesi Johnson and with Darcus Howe as host, people in the Caribbean are likely to speak in three or four registers depending on who you are speaking to: more familiar with family and friends, and more formally in public. As each Caribbean island has its own Patois too, for some people speaking the Patois of another island means they communicate in yet another register. As someone who speaks only basic French, it made me consider how many different versions of French are spoken around the world, how dominant English remains, and the positive and negative implications of that.

As a poet, I write from emotion, voice and form, often not considering the grammatical aspects until the final draft/s. So it has been interesting to note how much the translators considered how they would use the tools of poetry before applying them. Some translators aimed to capture a similar cadence to Awono's poem. The collaborative translation between Sarah Ardizzone and Rohan Ayinde—with Rohan being a spoken word specialist—meant that tools such as rhythm and onomatopoeia were probably more important than other tools, ensuring that their translation had the focus and tone which would be enhanced by its orality.

After reading this book it encouraged me to think about a poem differently in the sense of how many alternative readings people from different regions and backgrounds can bring to one poem, yet how the essence of the themes—such as childhood—remain the same. As I moved further into the book, I found myself reading the commentaries before the poem, so experiencing their approaches through different senses helped to shape a different poem, as it did with Nfor E. Njinyoh's poem in the shape of a fish trap. (Love it!). And so I dare myself to try and read "Le poème de Yambacongo" in Shetlandic.

Georgina Collins's innovative project has enabled me to view Awono's poem through a multipaned, multicoloured glass window which reflects the project curators background—her internationalism, her knowledge and her friendships. She has created something wonderful and fun here. I will select one of my poems, every now and then and consider how many ways it can be read, viewed and heard—the measure of a poem.

REFERENCES

Caribbean Nights: Poetry. Hosted by Darcus Howe. BBC 2, 14 June 1986.

Tunca, D. "Linguistic Counterpoint in Gbenga Agbenugba's Another Lonely Londoner". *Matatu -Frankfurt Then Amsterdam-*, vol. 36, 2009, pp. 195–214.

BIOGRAPHIES

Kareem James Abu-Zeid, PhD, is an Egyptian-American freelance translator of poets and novelists from across the Arab world, translating from Arabic, French and German. He has received the 2022 Sarah Maguire Prize for Poetry in Translation, a 2018 NEA translation grant, PEN Center USA's 2017 translation prize, *Poetry Magazine's* 2014 translation prize, a Fulbright research fellowship, and residencies from the Lannan Foundation and the Banff Center, among other honours. He is also author of the book *The Poetics of Adonis and Yves Bonnefoy: Poetry as Spiritual Practice*. The online hub for his work is www.kareemjamesabuzeid.com.

Jean Anderson recently retired from Te Herenga Waka / Victoria University of Wellington, where she founded the New Zealand Centre for Literary Translation in 2006. She has specialised in mainly prose texts from the Francophone Pacific (Chantal Spitz, Moetai Brotherson, Flora Aurima Devatine). She has also done a number of co-translations into French (Patricia Grace). She is particularly interested in supporting Indigenous writing.

JK Anowe (he/they) is an Igbo-born poet and MFA+MA candidate at the Litowitz Creative Writing Program. As a Gwendolyn M. Carter Fellow in African Studies at Northwestern University, Anowe lives and writes from somewhere in Chicago.

Sarah Ardizzone is an award-winning translator of some sixty titles from French. Her work spans hip-hop lyrics, memoir, picture books, graphic novels and literary fiction for all ages. Authors include Faïza Guène, Gaël Faye, Alain Mabanckou, Bessora, Yasmina Reza, Joann Sfar, Daniel Pennac and Alexandre Dumas. Twice recipient of the Marsh award and the Scott Moncrieff prize, in 2022 she was appointed Chevalier de l'Ordre des Arts et des Lettres.

Jean-Claude Awono (see last page).

Rohan Ayinde is an interdisciplinary artist and poet based between London and Chicago. His work traverses audio, visual and literary forms and embraces installation and performance. He is one half of the wayward/motile collaborative duo i.as.in.we, with friend/producer/dancer Yewande YoYo Odunubi. He received his MA in Visual and Critical Studies from the School of the Art Institute of Chicago (2019) and is Director of Blanc gallery (Chicago). He is currently co-directing *iwoyi* (with Tayo Rapoport), a 5-screen-installation for *Beyond the Bassline: 500 years of Black British Music* (British Library, 2024).

Georgina Collins (see last page).

Bonnie Chau is a writer, translator, and occasional artist from Southern California, whose short story collection *All Roads Lead to Blood* was a 2019 CLMP (Community of Literary Magazines and Presses) Firecracker Award finalist. She holds an MFA in fiction and literary translation from Columbia University, and has received support from Kundiman, Art Farm Nebraska, Vermont Studio Center, Millay Colony, the Black Mountain Institute and the Stadler Center. She is currently an editor at *4Columns, Public Books*, and the *Evergreen Review*, an adjunct professor at Columbia and Fordham University, and a board member of the American Literary Translators Association.

Kadija Sesay is a Sierra Leonean/British scholar and activist. She has edited several anthologies and was Publisher of SABLE LitMag for 15 years. The magazine included an In Translation section. She has published her own creative work including a poetry collection titled *Irki*. She is founder of the first International Black Speculative Writing Festival, co-founder of Mboka Festival and founder of the 'AfriPoeTree' app. She has received awards and fellowships for her work in the creative arts and judged several prizes. In her ongoing collaborative project between SABLE LitMag and Mboka Festival, classic works by African writers are translated into Gambian languages. Such texts include Linton Kwesi Johnson's poems and *The Upright Revolution* by Ngugi wa Thiong'o.

John T. Gilmore has lived and worked in Barbados and England. He has worked in advertising, journalism and cultural administration, as well as being an academic who has taught a wide range of subjects, including Caribbean and European History, French, Translation Studies, and English Literature. He is currently a Professor in the Department of English and Comparative Literary Studies at the University of Warwick. His many publications include the volume on *Satire* in the New Critical Idiom series (Routledge, 2017), and a verse translation, from the Latin, of Guillaume Massieu, *Coffee: A Poem* (ARC Publications, 2019).

Khadijah Sanusi Gumbi is a lecturer at Bayero University Kano and visiting scholar at Maryam Abacha American University of Nigeria. Her expertise in International Relations is enriched by overseas experience in the United States, United Kingdom, Saudi Arabia and Switzerland, as well as a portfolio of scholarly articles. Beyond academia, Khadijah is an Active Citizens' facilitator, advocating for education and mentorship. Founder of MECIN Consult Ltd, she spearheads initiatives in mentorship, coaching and inspiration.

Sophie Herxheimer is a London-based artist and poet. Her work has been shown at her local allotments, Tate Modern and on a giant mural along the sea-front at Margate. She's held many residencies in the UK and internationally. Her collection *Velkom to Inklandt* (Short Books, 2017) was a Sunday Times Book of the Year. Her book *60 Lovers to Make and Do*, (Henningham Family Press, 2019) was a TLS Book of the Year. Her latest collection is *INDEX* (zimZalla, 2021), a box of 78 collage poems, made from found text, published as a deck of prophetic cards.

N. Kamala is a retired Professor of French at Jawaharlal Nehru University, New Delhi (specialising in Translation Studies). She received the Katha Award for Translation in 1998. Her publications include an English translation of Toru Dutt's French novel *The Diary of Mademoiselle d'Arvers* (Penguin, 2005), an edited book, *Translating Women: Indian Interventions* (Zubaan, 2009), and an edited anthology of translations of Indian women's writings into French, entitled *Shakti. Quand les Indiennes ont leur mot à écrire* (Goyal, 2013). She has also co-edited two volumes of translations of contemporary short stories from mainly lesser-known Indian languages into French: *Rangoli. Anthologie de nouvelles indiennes contemporaines.* (Goyal, 2018).

Christine De Luca writes in English and Shaetlan (Shetlandic), her mother tongue. She was appointed Edinburgh's Makar (poet laureate) for 2014-2017. Her eighth poetry collection *Veeve*, was published by Mariscat Press, Edinburgh (2021). She also enjoys translation and has had five bilingual volumes published (in French, Italian, Icelandic, Norwegian and English). De Luca has also worked with musicians and visual artists: her most recent poetry collaboration is *Another Time, Another Place* with Victoria Crowe (Scottish Gallery, 2021). In addition, she has written and translated stories for children and published a second novel: *The Trials of Mary Johnsdaughter* (Luath Press: Edinburgh, 2022).

Prudence Lucha was born in 1971. She hails from Bamunka-Ndop, a village in the Ngoketunjia Division of the North West Region of Cameroon. She has a Master's Degree in Translation from the Advanced School of Translators and Interpreters at the University of Buea. She is currently working as a Senior Translator in the Translation Unit of the Ministry of Transport, Yaounde-Cameroon. She translated Alphonsius Ategha's novel, *Clandestin sur son propre Continent* (published by L'Harmattan) into English as *Stranger on his Continent*.

Maneo Refiloe Mohale is a queer South African editor, feminist writer and poet. Their work has appeared in various local and international publications, including Jalada, Prufrock, The Johannesburg Review of Books, and others. Mohale was Bitch Media's first Global Feminism Writing Fellow in their inaugural 2016 class, where they wrote on race, media, sexuality and survivorship. They have been long-listed twice for the Sol Plaatje European Union Poetry Anthology Award, and their debut collection of poetry, *Everything is a Deathly Flower* was published with uHlanga Press in September 2019. In 2020, they were shortlisted for the Ingrid Jonker Poetry Prize, the youngest finalist of that year. In 2021, *Everything is a Deathly Flower* won the Glenna Luschei Prize for African Poetry.

Nfor E. Njinyoh is a translator and editor. He holds a Master of Arts in Translation from the Advanced School of Translators and Interpreters (ASTI), Buea. He is an alumnus of the Bakwa-Bristol Literary Translation Workshop and co-editor of the bilingual anthology *Your Feet Will Lead You Where Your Heart Is/Le Crépuscule des âmes sœurs*. His short story translations have appeared in the aforementioned anthology and in *Bakwa 11: When Love Is a Scream*. He may or may not be working on a collection of his poems.

Mary Noonan grew up in Cork, Ireland, where she now lives. She teaches French literature at University College Cork, specialising in the work of French women playwrights, French film and poetry. She also teaches the translation of poetry. She has published two poetry collections: *The Fado House* (Dedalus Press, 2012) and *Stone Girl* (Dedalus Press, 2019).

Aileen Ruane is an Assistant Professor of French at Grove City College in Pennsylvania where she teaches French language, literatures and translation. Prior to her appointment at GCC, she was an FRQSC (Fonds de recherche du Québec – Société et culture)-funded postdoctoral fellow at Concordia University in Montreal, researching feminist ethics and politics of translation between Ireland and Quebec. She holds a doctorate in Études littéraires from Université Laval in Quebec, and an MA in French studies from the University of Illinois at Urbana-Champaign. Prior to returning to academia, she worked as a professional actor in Northeast Ohio and Chicago.

Alyssa Salzberg is a PhD student at Trinity College of Dublin, where she is studying themes of sexuality in French/English translations of Interwar French Surrealist literature. She has a Master's degree in Translation Studies from University College Cork, where she studied French and Japanese translation. She also has a BA in English Literature with a minor in Japanese from Mount Holyoke College in South Hadley, Massachusetts. She is originally from Baltimore, Maryland in the United States, and she has lived in Philadelphia and Kyoto, Japan. She is a poet and writer, and plans to continue pursuing literary translation.

Stephanie Smee is an Australian translator living in Sydney who left a career in the law to pursue her passion for languages. She works as a literary translator mainly from French, although she has also worked from Swedish, co-translating with her Swedish mother. Recent publications include translations of Hélène Gaudy's *A World with No Shore*, Hannelore Cayre's *The Godmother*, winner of the International Dagger for translated crime fiction, and a New York Times *Notable Book of 2019*, Françoise Frenkel's rediscovered WWII memoir, *No Place to Lay One's Head*, awarded the JQ-Wingate Prize *2019*, and Joseph Ponthus' prose poem, *On the Line – Notes from a factory*.

Elizabeth (Betty) Wilson is a former head of the Department of French, University of the West Indies, Kingston, Jamaica. Co-editor of the first anthology of writing by Caribbean women, her translations include the novels *Juletane* (Myriam Warner-Vieyra, Waveland Press, 2014), Gisèle Pineau's *Exile, according to Julia* (University of Virginia Press, 2003) and stories by Yanick Lahens: *Aunt Resia and the Spirits and Other Stories* (University of Virginia Press, 2010). She was awarded the Palmes Académiques by the government of France for her contribution to the teaching of French Language and Literature, and was a Senior Fulbright Fellow at Radcliffe College, 1989.

ACKNOWLEDGEMENTS

Needless to say, this publication would not have come about without the inspiration and support of certain key people. My deepest thanks go to Jean-Claude Awono, who has always gone out of his way to help me as a creative, and without his talent, this book would not have become a reality. I'd also like to thank Dzekashu MacViban and Nfor E. Njinyoh at Bakwa, who were willing to embrace my idea and give me the encouragement and creative scope to run with it, and without restraint! Thanks also to Prof. Madhu Krishnan and Prof. Ruth Bush at the University of Bristol who, over a number of projects, have brought together like-minded people, passionate about creative Africa, inspiring the conversations and relationships that lead to projects such as this one. In addition, I have to thank Madhu for making me part of the European Research Council-funded project, Literary Activism in sub-Saharan Africa: Commons, Publics and Networks of Practice (LITCOM), which has supported and partly financed this publication. Alongside Madhu and over many trips to Africa and some within Europe, I was given the opportunity to meet a number of people instrumental in this book. And so, I must thank all the wonderful writers, translators, academics, publishers, artists of all kinds, who have nourished my life and this publication. There are too many to mention, but I cannot forget the time, the fun, and enriching conversations I have enjoyed with Edwige Dro, Mariette Tchamda Mbunpi and Maryberth Aseh. Thanks too to the empowering Kadija Sesay who I initially "met" through poetry when she wrote the preface to my first book, *The Other Half of History* in 2007, and who knows if she has written the Afterword to my last! In fact, I must extend my gratitude to all the patient and talented contributors to this volume. We did it! 19 distinct ways of translating Awono. And most importantly, thank you to Mark, who has embraced all of my travelling, the tiredness, the happiness, the juggling jobs and the poetry in our lives.

❧❦

Jean-Claude Awono is a poet, teacher, editor and publisher. He studied French at the University of Yaounde I before focusing on the teaching of language and literature at the university's École Normale Supérieure.

Over the years, Awono's passion for poetry has taken him down many different cultural and literary pathways. He created, with colleagues, *La Ronde des Poètes du Cameroun* (The Poetry Circle of Cameroon), which served as a springboard for his literary career. It also led to some of the capital's key literary and cultural events: the opening of Yaounde's *Francis Bebey Cultural Centre* and that of the *Cameroonian Observatory of Culture*, as well as the launch of the *Rondine Poetry Prize* and the unveiling of Yaounde's *'Seven Hills' International Poetry Festival*. With regard to publishing, Awono was Series Editor at *Éditions Clé* before starting up the publishing house, *Éditions de la Ronde* which, in 2007, became part of *Éditions Ifrikiya*, where he has been Director since 2011.

Awono's role as an editor and poet has taken him all over the world, from France to China, Canada and Côte d'Ivoire. He has won Cameroon's prestigious *Order of Merit* and *Order of Valour*, as well as distinctions for his poetry: the *International Poetry Prize of Bretagne-Réunie* (2011), Senegal's *David Diop International Poetry Prize* (2019) and Canada's *Fernando d'Alméida International Poetry Prize* (2020). He is a literary consultant, has judged numerous literary prizes, and this year, his poetry collection, *A hauteur de sang (At Blood Level)* was on the Cameroonian school syllabus. Since 2016, Awono has been the traditional chief of the Mbam-et-Inoubou department of Cameroon.

❧❦

Dr Georgina Collins is a Freelance Literary Translator, Writer, and Literary Translation Consultant at the University of Bristol. She also runs her own ceramics studio, *Iremía Pottery* in Warwickshire, England. Collins has an MA and PhD from Warwick University and has worked as a Lecturer in Translation Studies at the Universities of Glasgow and Warwick.

Georgina is passionate about poetry and in 2007, she produced the first ever French-English bilingual collection of Francophone African women's poetry, entitled *The Other Half of History*. The foreword was written by Kadija Sesay. Collins has also translated the poetry of Jean-Claude Awono and Senegalese author Mame Seck Mbacké for *Modern Poetry in Translation* (2021; 2016), as well as the activist poetry of French writer Laura Boullic for *Active Art* (Paraguay Press, 2019). In 2021, Collins took third place in the Stephen Spender Prize for poetry translation with another text by Awono.

Georgina has published a number of academic and professional articles on the translation of Francophone African texts and in 2022, she judged the Scott Moncrieff Prize (from the Society of Authors and Translators Association) for literary translation from French. She has translated the literary works of West African writers such as Sokhna Benga and Felwine Sarr (both from Senegal) and translated books by French writers such as Monica Sabolo and Lauren Bastide for Macmillan and Penguin respectively. In 2013, Georgina won a joint English Pen Award for Writing in Translation for her contribution to *Writing Revolution: The Voices from Tunis to Damascus* (I.B. Tauris).

Sign up for our newsletter at www.bakwabooks.com and receive exclusive updates, including extracts, podcasts, event notifications, discounts, competitions and giveaways.

Follow Bakwa Books

X: @BakwaBooks
Instagram: @BakwaBooks
Facebook: @BakwaBooks

www.ingramcontent.com/pod-product-compliance
Lightning Source LLC
Chambersburg PA
CBHW071121160426
43196CB00013B/2666